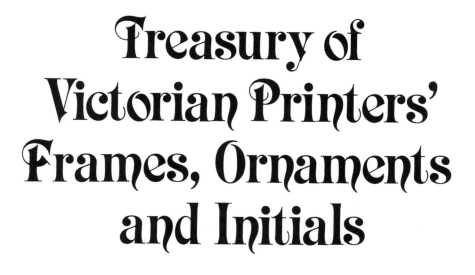

Treasury of Victorian Printers' Frames, Ornaments and Initials

Edited by

Carol Belanger Grafton

Dover Publications, Inc.

New York

Copyright © 1984 by Dover Publications, Inc.
All rights reserved under Pan American and International Copyright Conventions.

Published in Canada by General Publishing Company, 30 Lesmill Road, Don Mills, Toronto, Ontario.
Published in the United Kingdom by Constable and Company, Ltd.

Treasury of Victorian Printers' Frames, Ornaments and Initials is a new work, first published by Dover Publications, Inc., in 1984. The designs were selected and arranged by Carol Belanger Grafton from *The Printers' International Specimen Exchange*, Volumes IV, V and VI (London: Office of the Paper and Printing Trades Journal, 1883, 1884, 1885). The Publisher's Note was prepared specially for this edition. The publisher thanks Howard Garrett for making the set of *The Printers' International Specimen Exchange* available for the preparation of this volume.

DOVER *Pictorial Archive* SERIES

Manufactured in the United States of America
Dover Publications, Inc., 31 East 2nd Street, Mineola, N.Y. 11501

Library of Congress Cataloging in Publication Data

Main entry under title:

Treasury of Victorian printers' frames, ornaments, and initials.

(Dover pictorial archive series)
"Designs were selected . . . from The Printers' international specimen exchange, volumes IV, V, and VI (London : Office of the Paper and Printing Trades journal, 1883, 1884, 1885)"—P.
1. Printers' ornaments. 2. Printing—Specimens. 3. Type ornaments. 4. Printing—History—19th century. I. Grafton, Carol Belanger. II. Printers' international specimen exchange. III. Series.
Z250.3.T73 1984   686.2′24   84-8023
ISBN 0-486-24703-1 (pbk.)

Publisher's Note

During Queen Victoria's 64-year reign, the art of printing underwent major technological changes. Numerous new processes were introduced and the mechanization, first of presswork and later of composition and platemaking, allowed the mass production of all kinds of printed matter. Within this period, the printing trades were transformed from crafts involving a great deal of handwork to industries dominated by machinery. At the same time, the demands of commerce in this golden age of advertising, together with the tastes of the rising bourgeois class, had a marked effect on typography and graphic design. The esthetic standards of printers generally suffered as a result of these sweeping changes both in the workplace and in the marketplace, although some leaders in the field sought to counter the decline in artistry by encouraging good design and technique by a form of peer review.

The Printers' International Specimen Exchange was one of the most interesting and productive efforts in this direction. Organized by Andrew Tuer (1838–1900), the *Exchange* was published annually from 1880 until 1895. Contributions were invited from "practical letterpress and lithographic printers, managers of printing offices, compositors, pressmen and apprentices" who subscribed to the *Exchange* at the cost of one shilling a year. All subscribers were eligible to submit examples of their best work in a specified number of copies (which increased as the series gained popularity) to be judged on artistic and technical merits and included, if suitable, in the year's compilation. The *Exchange* attracted contributions from all over the British Empire, Western Europe and America. The specimen sheets, generally uniform in size but wonderfully varied in paper stock and style of execution, were collated and bound (for an additional charge) for the subscribers, who could then examine the production of many of their most skillful peers around the world.

Most of the subscribers specialized in "job" or general commercial printing. Their work included trade and consumer advertisements, menus, banknotes, invitations, letterheads, posters, catalogs, maps, broadsides, certificates, book covers, programs, cards, calendars, labels and so on. The specimens for the *Exchange* were usually printed in several colors, with a lavish use of gold and other metallic inks. Typographically, the designs show the eclecticism of their era. There is hardly a page among the hundreds in the three volumes used for the present collection (IV, 1883; V, 1884; VI, 1885) that is not richly adorned with frames and borders in high Victorian style.

The engravers and type founders of the Victorian age drew upon the entire Western (and to a lesser extent, Oriental) heritage of ornamental styles, and often combined them in novel ways. The examples of border treatments collected here incorporate fretwork, diaper patterns, foliated and floriated decoration and many other ornamental devices. Some of the designs incorporate scenic vignettes, religious and mythological subjects, naturalistic images of plants and animals, and the like. Scattered among the various enclosures are over 200 separate ornaments — fleurons, dingbats, head- and tail-pieces, and practically every other kind of graphic embellishment. There are also almost 50 decorative initials in a variety of styles.

To appreciate the technical achievements these compositions represent, it should be recalled that the plates were either engraved on wood or metal or laboriously set up in foundry type ornaments, piece borders and brass rules, intricate work indeed considering the media involved. The designs that were executed in two or more colors are in nearly perfect register. Reproduced here as they are in one color, it is almost impossible to tell that most of the sheets were pulled through the press at least twice.

The mechanical requirements of locking up the chase to hold all the elements in position for letterpress printing imposed a practical limitation on the arrangement of metal type, cuts and blocks, so most of the frames are rectilinear. There are occasional diagonal elements, and frequent use of corner cuts of various shapes tends to relieve the otherwise uniform geometry. One example of the latter is the spiderweb motif that recurs on at least four pages of this book. Thanks to modern photoreproduction methods, today's users of this material can treat the impressions so painstakingly achieved a century ago as "clip art," cutting and rearranging segments as needed for original compositions.

Writing about the *Exchange* in *Victorian Book Design and Colour Printing* (1972), Ruari McLean (who edited and introduced *The Noah's Ark A.B.C. and 8 Other Victorian Alphabet Books in Color*, Dover, 1976, 23355-3) has said: "Its influence was more in the field of jobbing than of book printing, but its pages are a good place to study the extraordinary things printers had quite suddenly become capable of designing." The frames, ornaments and initials selected by Carol Belanger Grafton, whose sensitivity to the needs of contemporary graphic designers has made her name practically synonymous with the Dover Pictorial Archive Series, are not only worthy of study as examples of the finest Victorian fancy printing, but are immediately usable, ready to reproduce and copyright-free.

1

F.C.

3

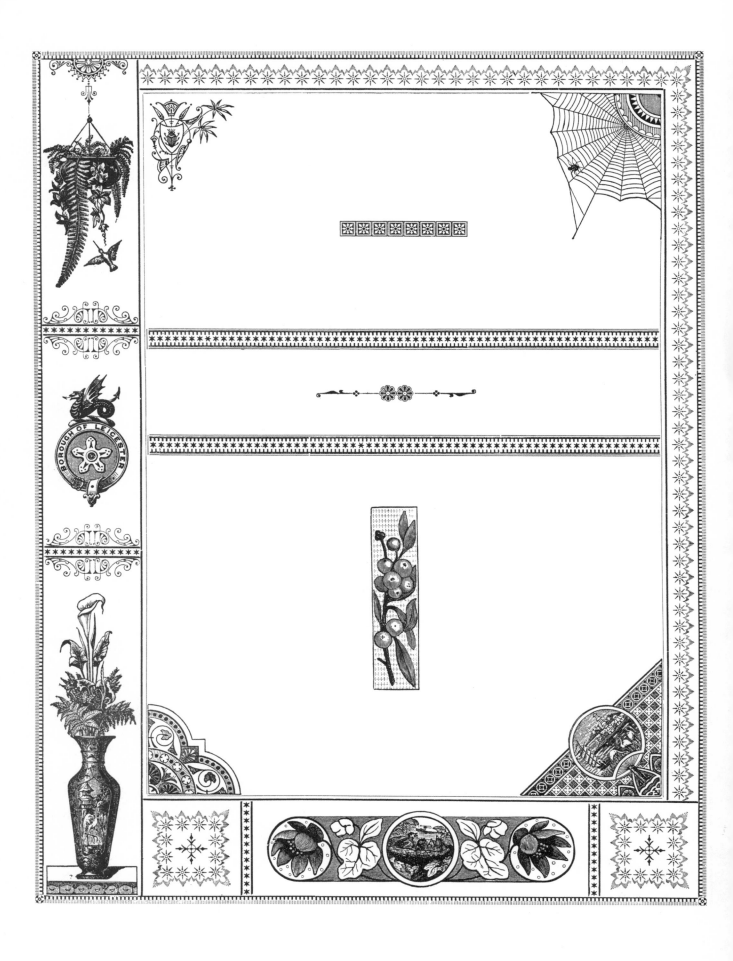

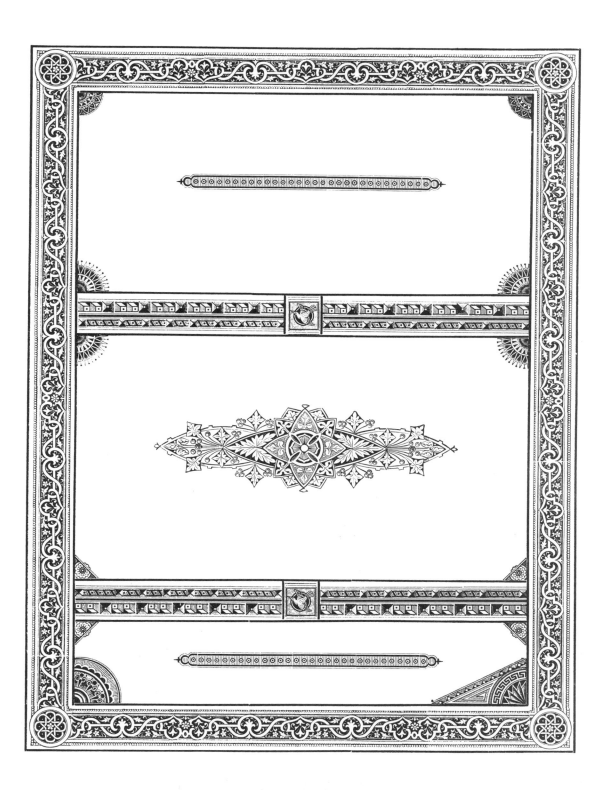

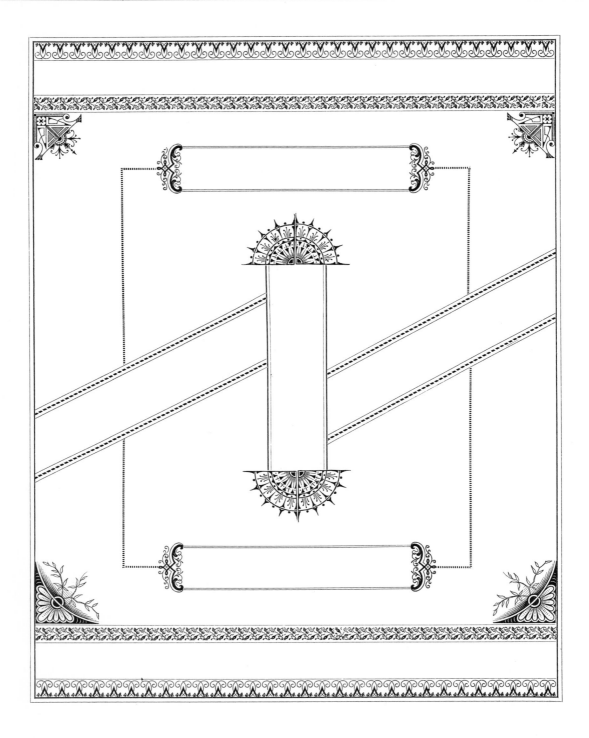

7

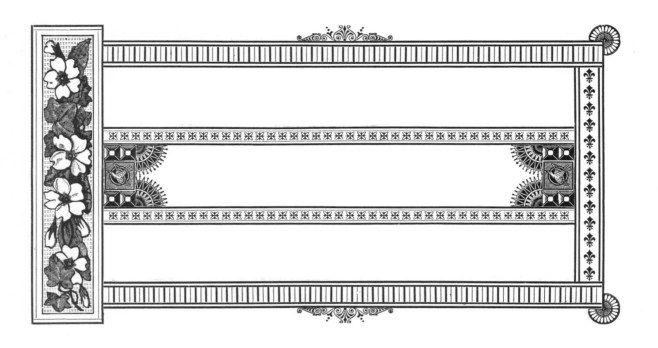

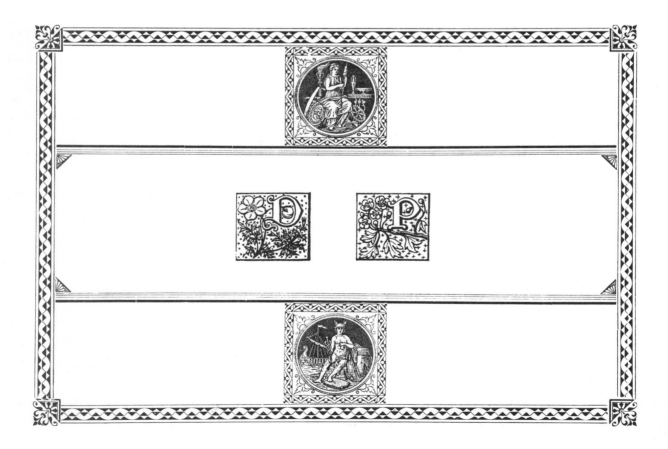

9

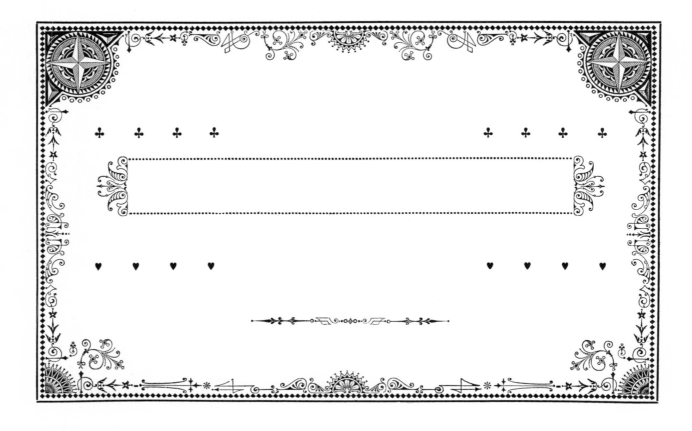

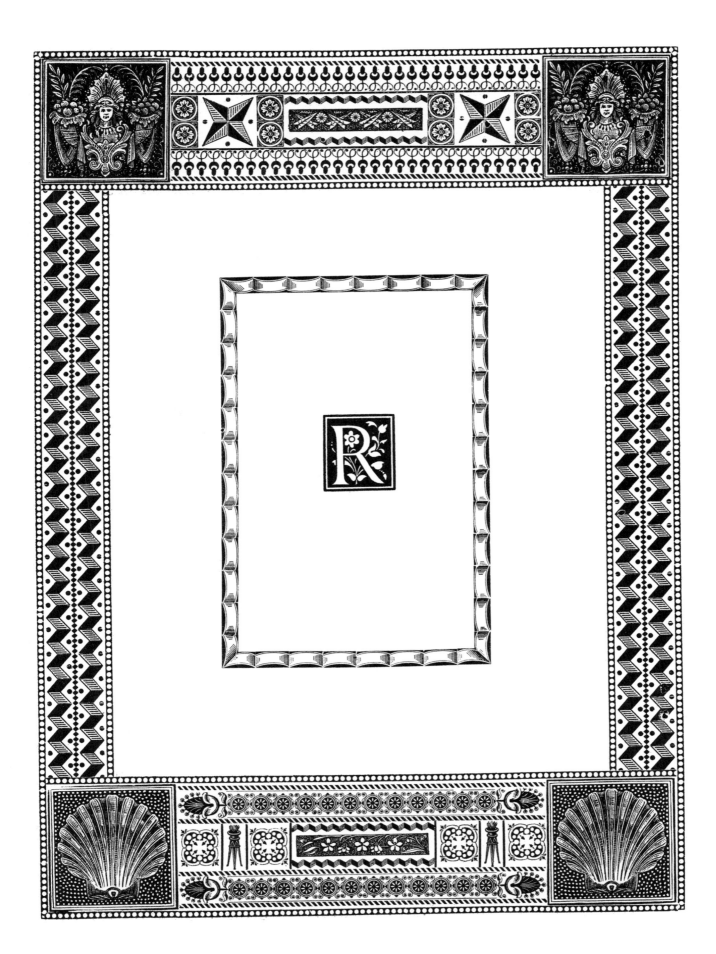

11

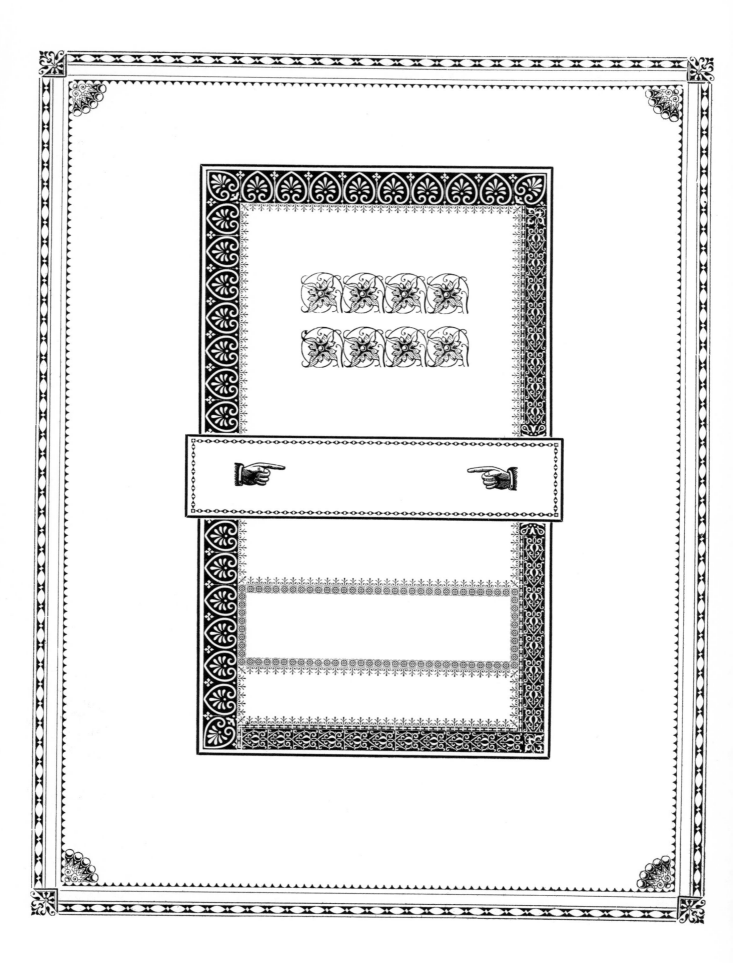

12

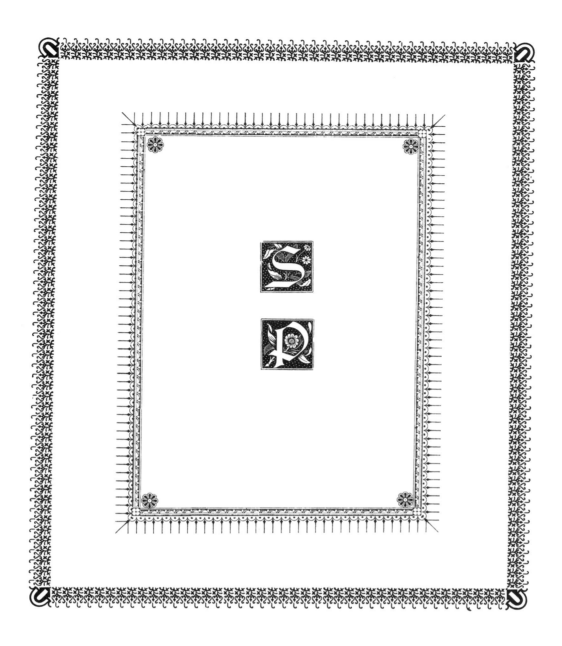

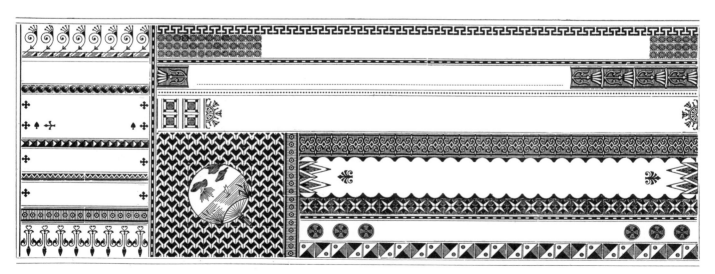

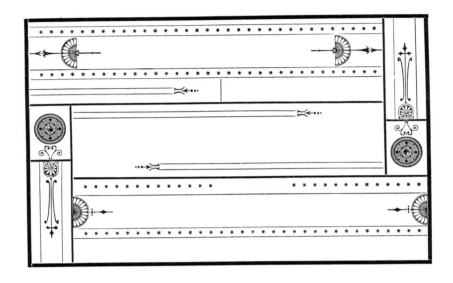

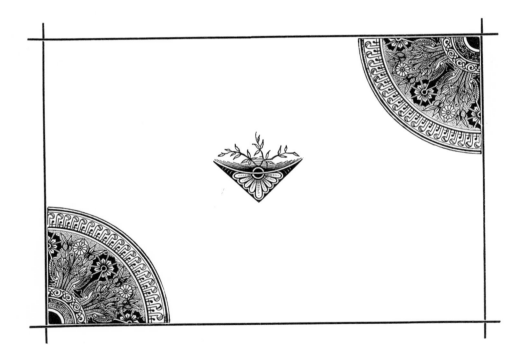

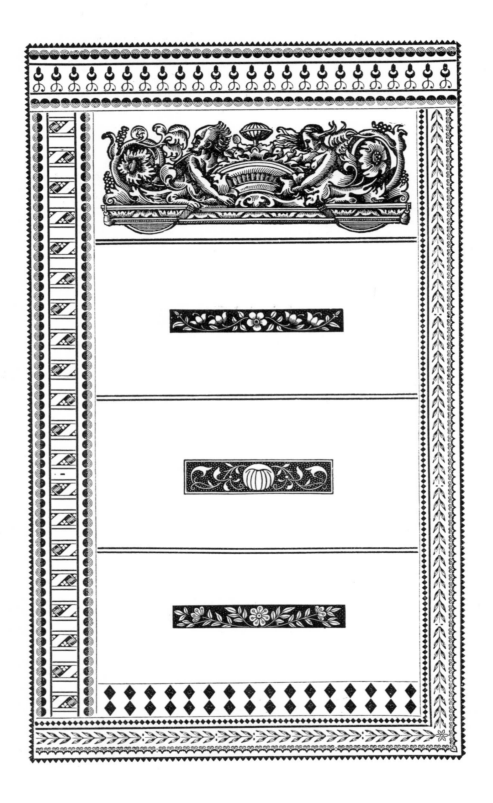

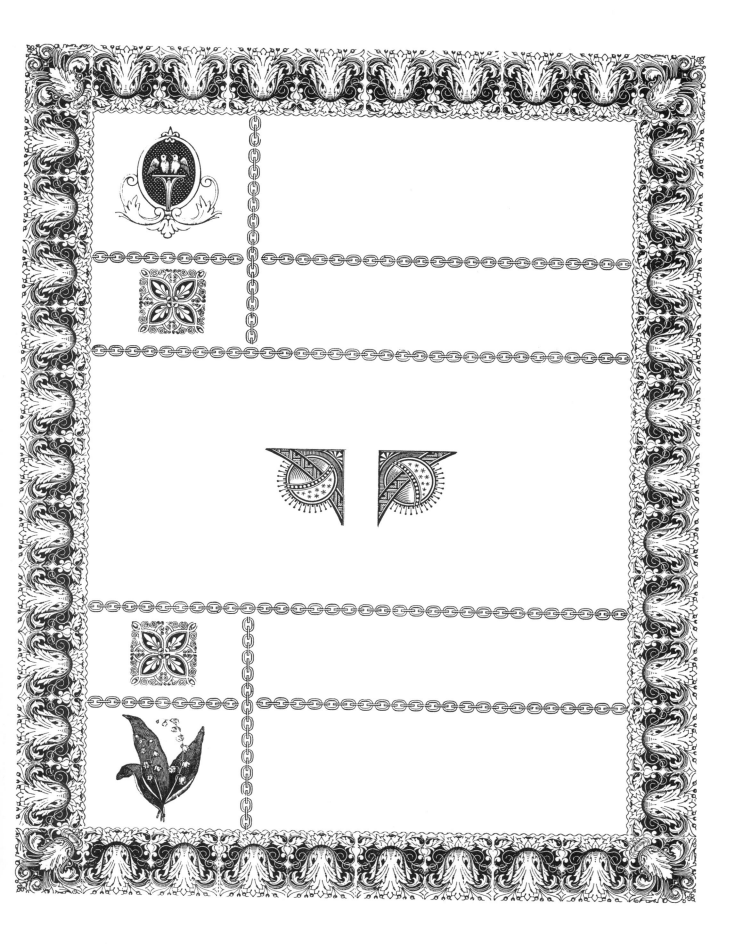

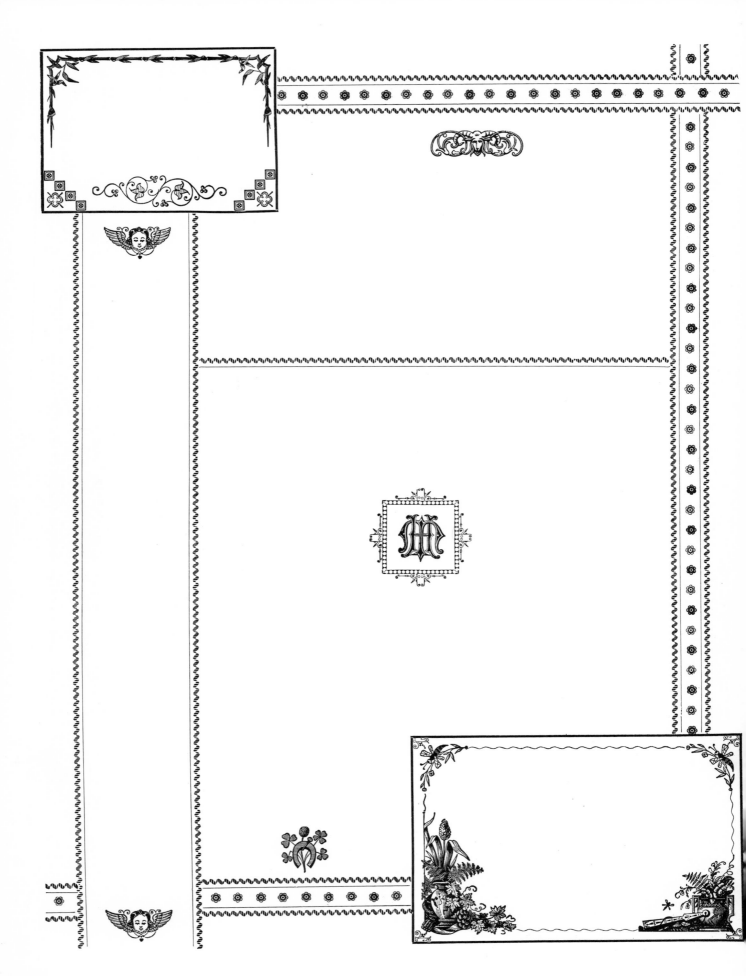

18

19

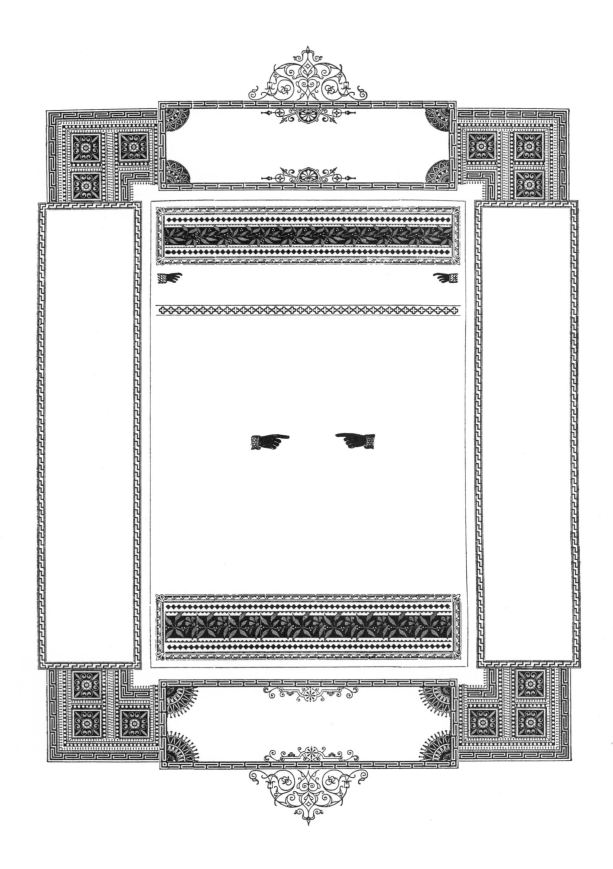

21

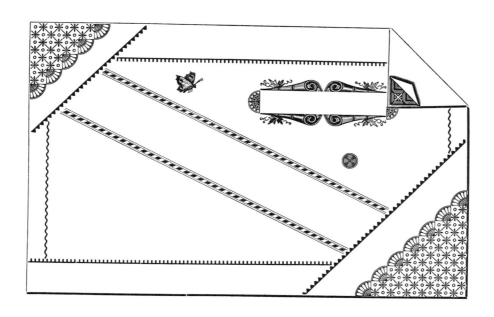

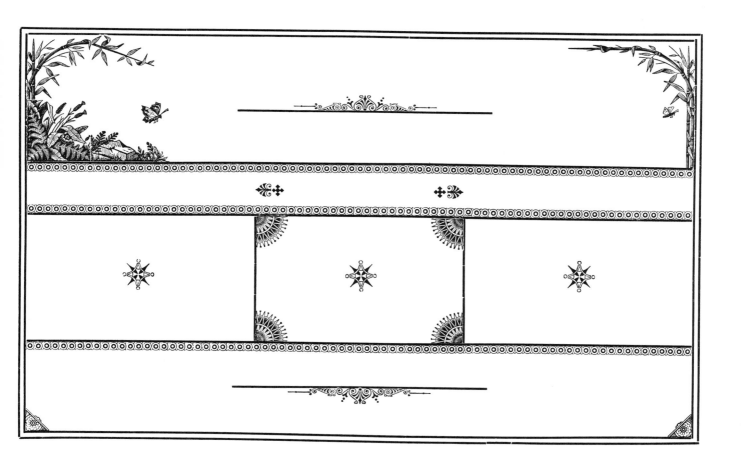

23

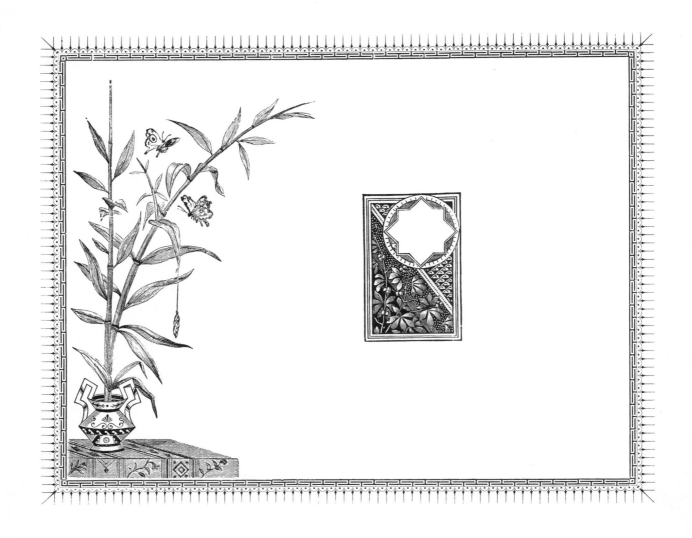

25

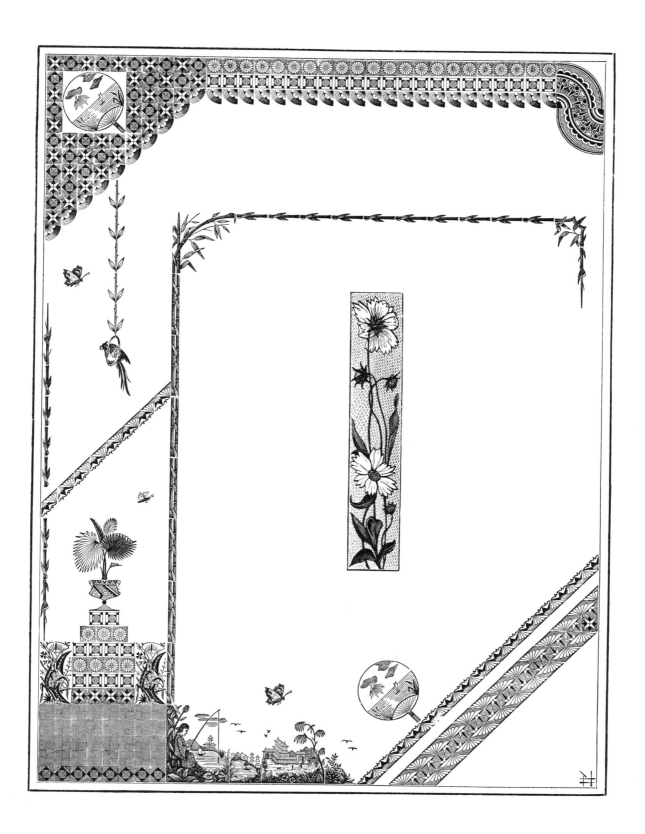

27

28

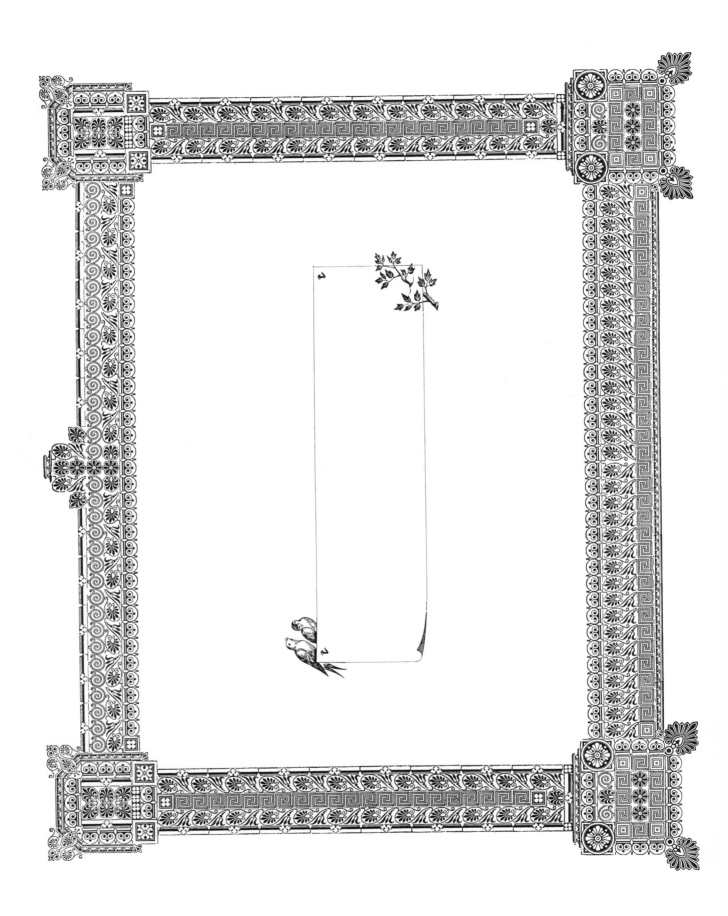

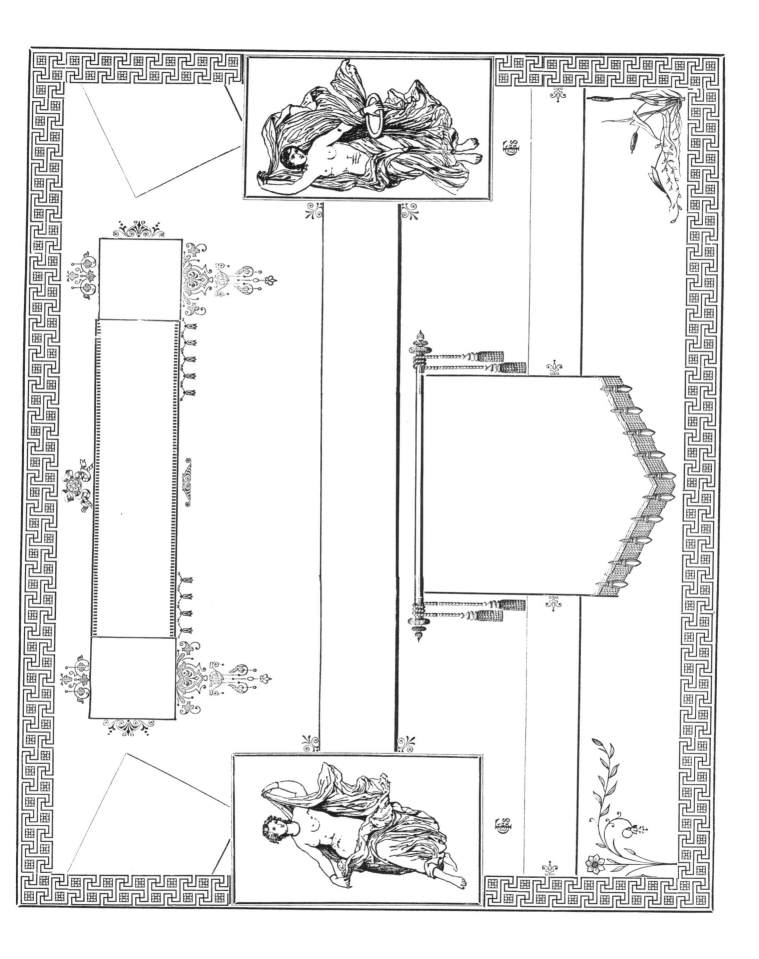

33

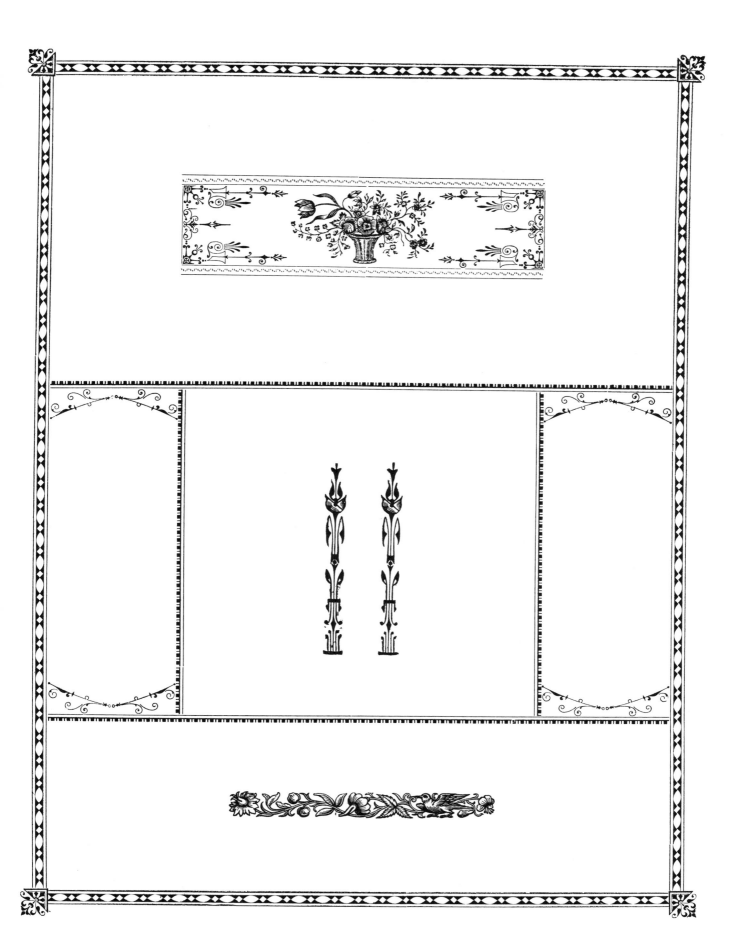

35

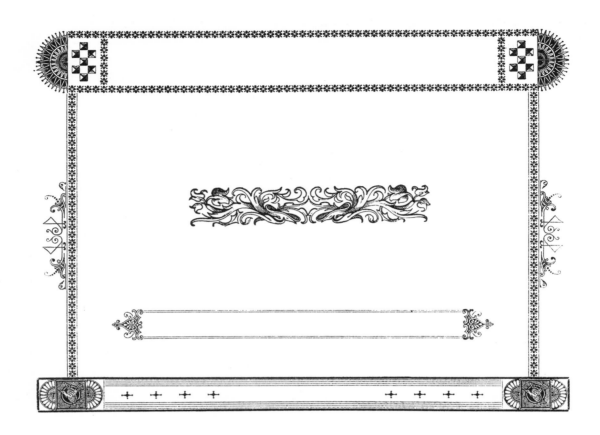

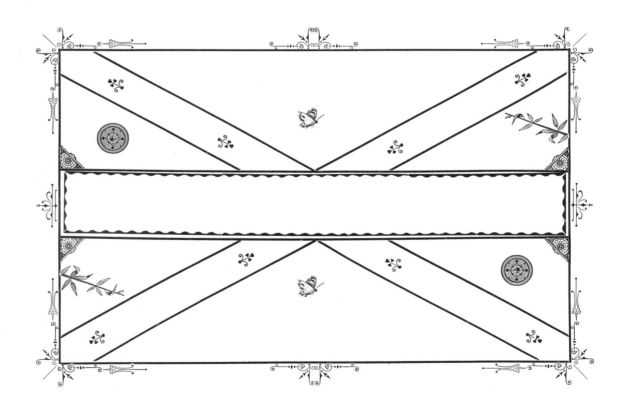

37

38

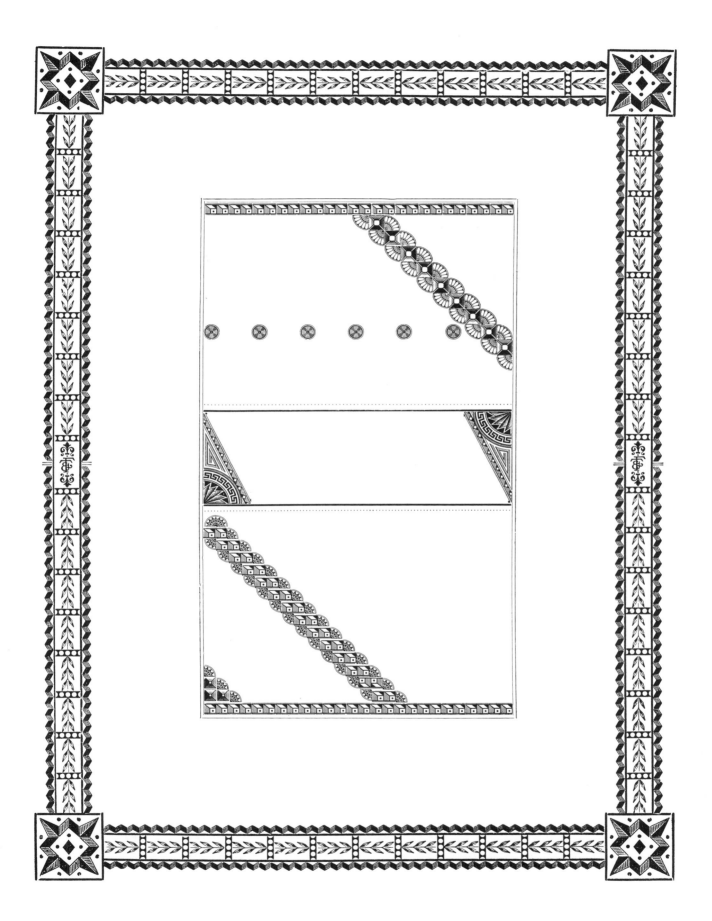

45

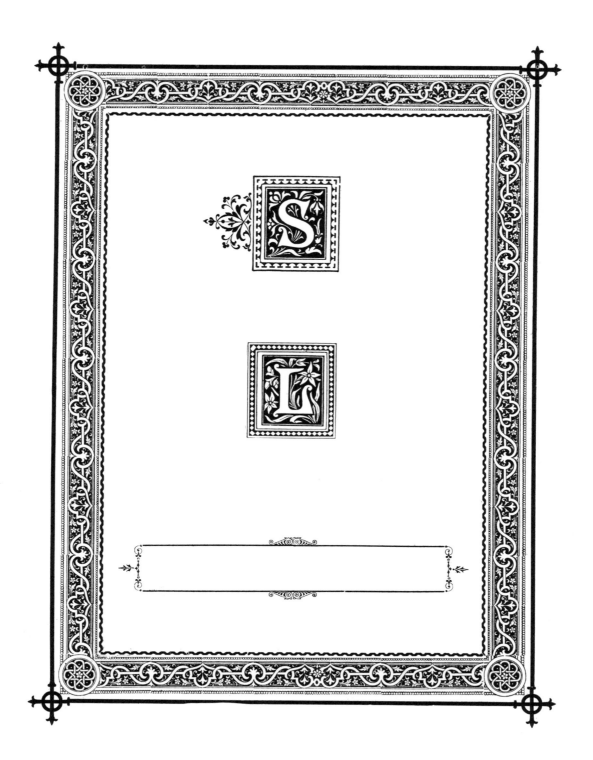

47

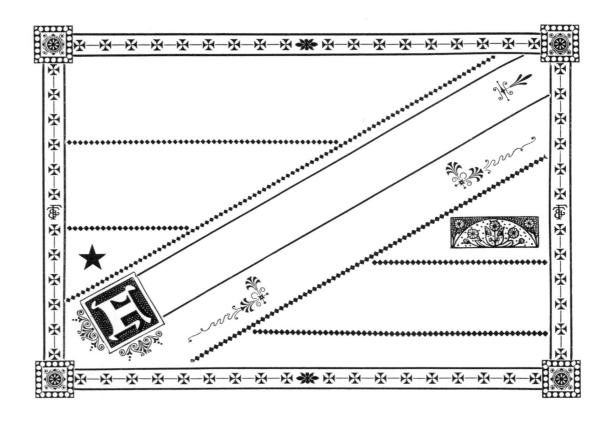

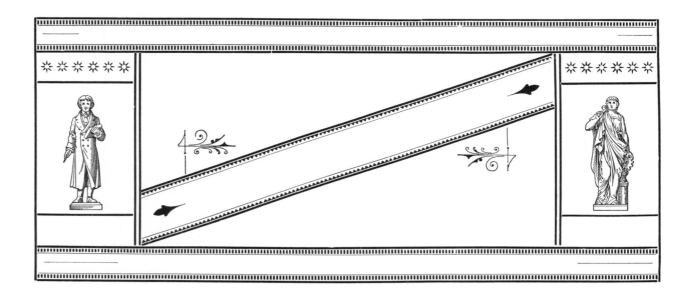

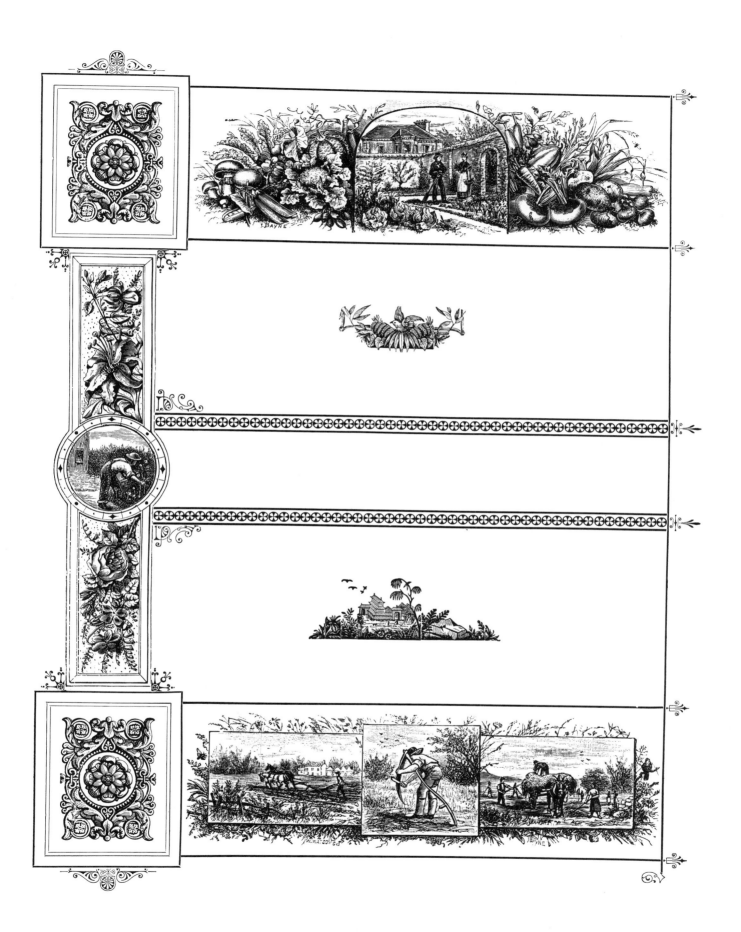

54

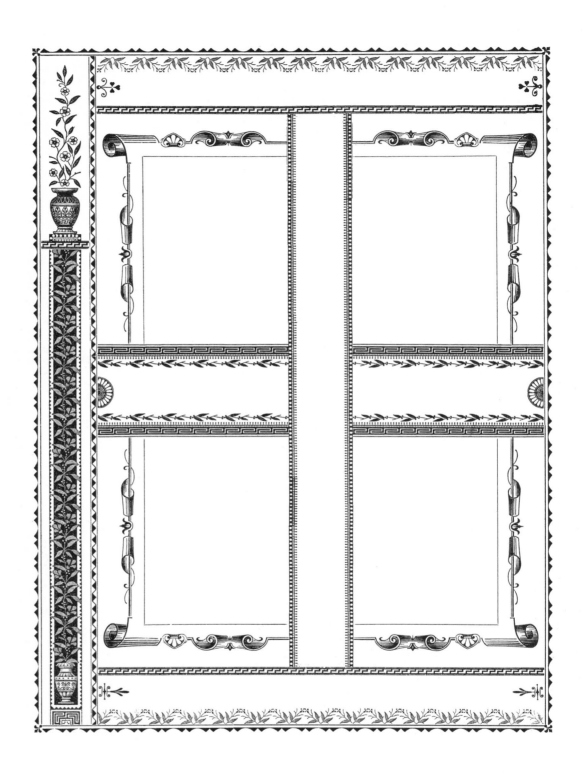

59

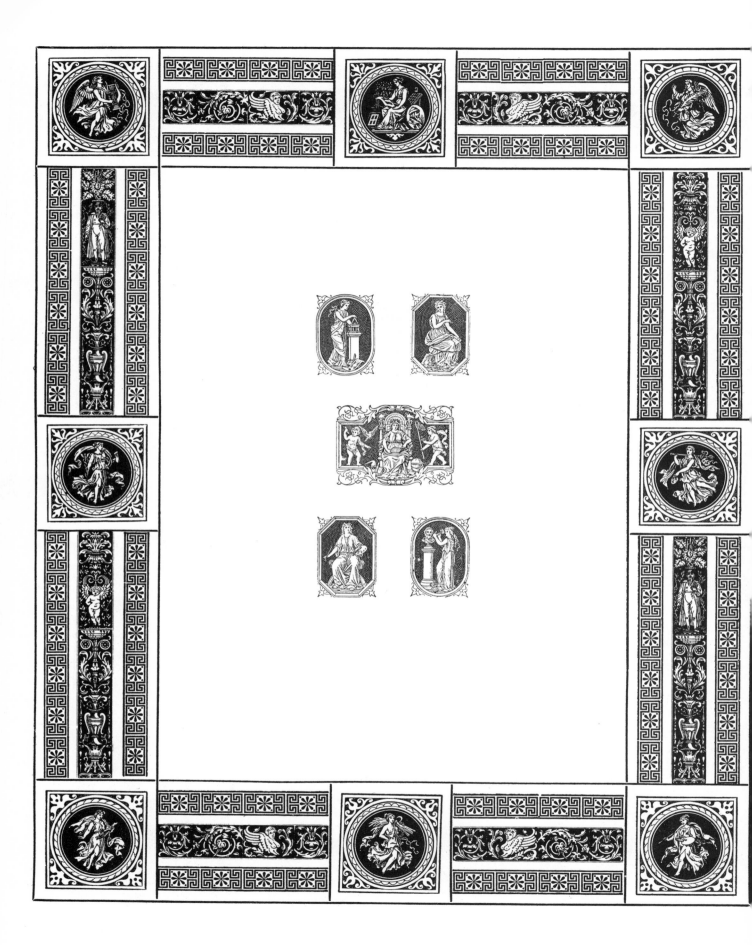

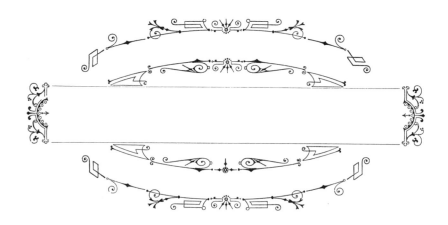

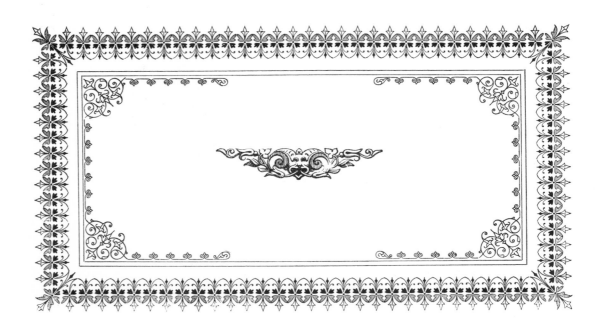

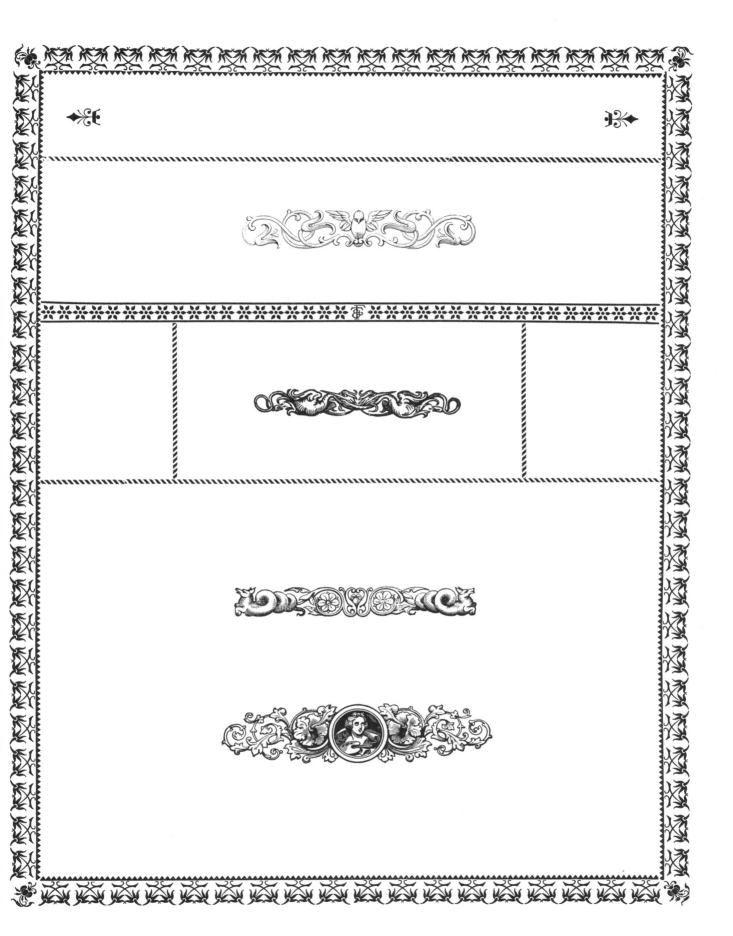

74

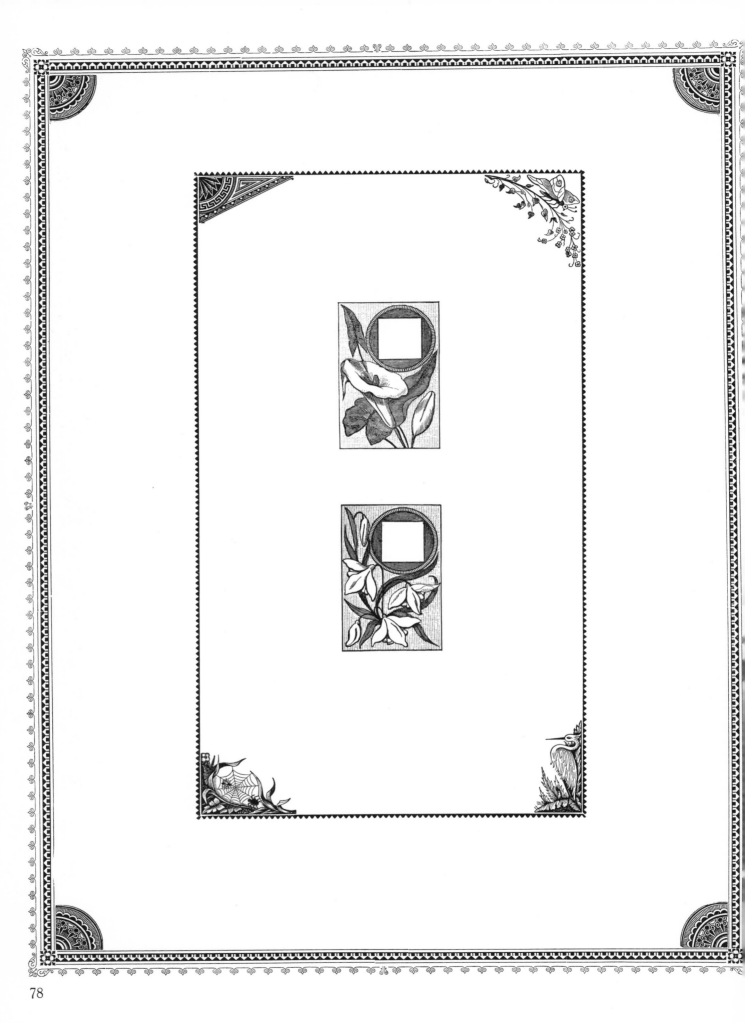

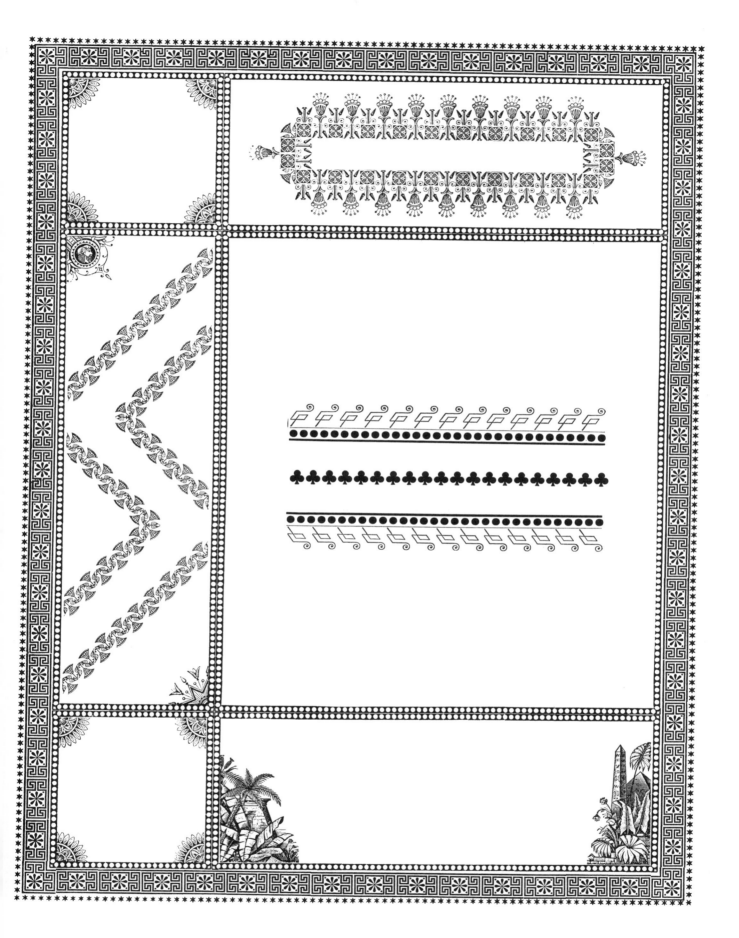

79

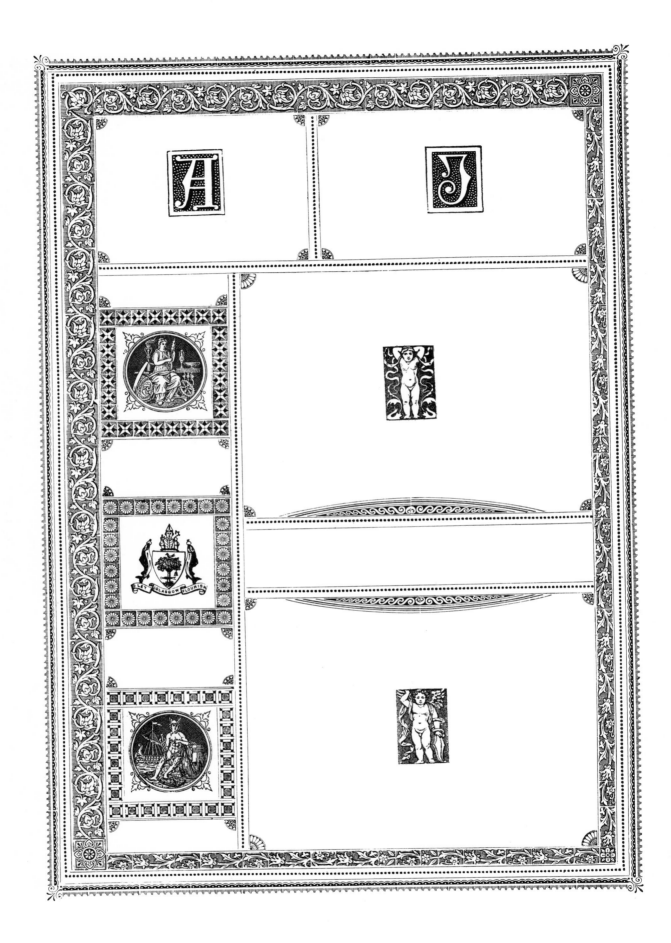

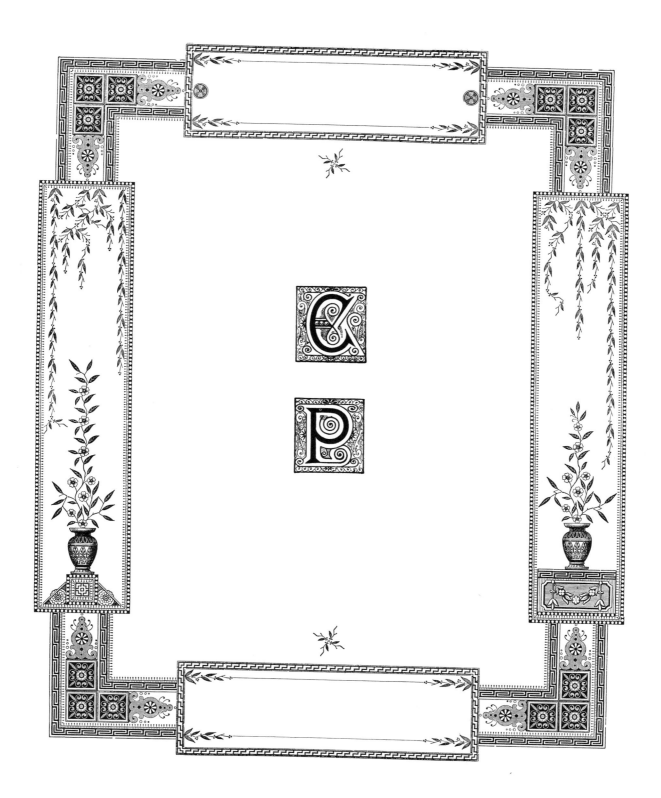

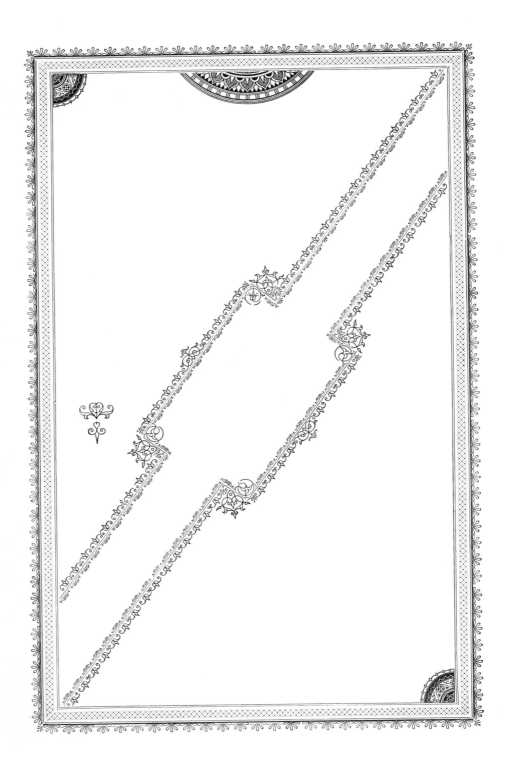

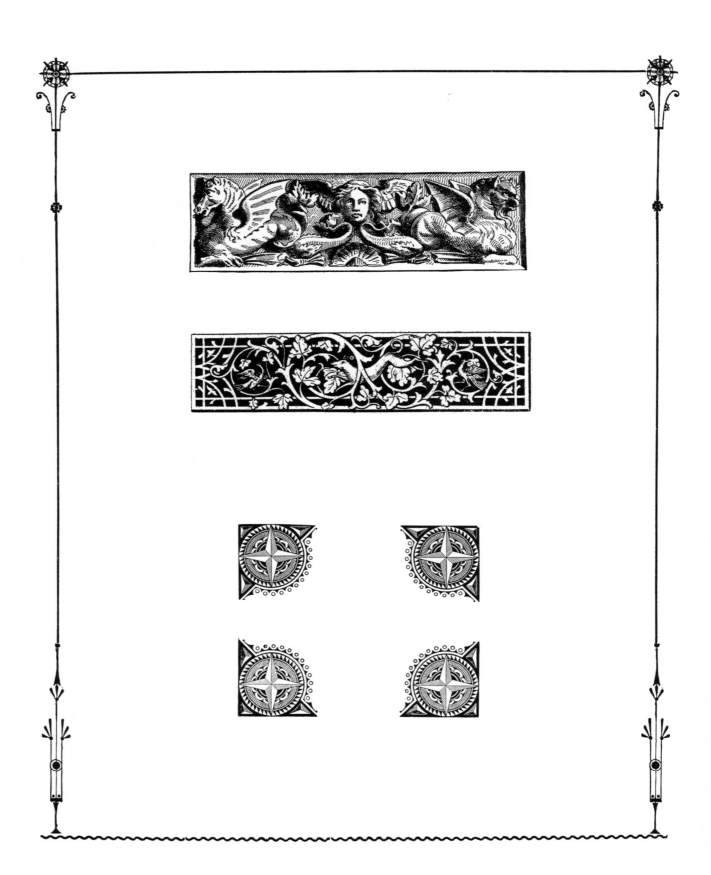

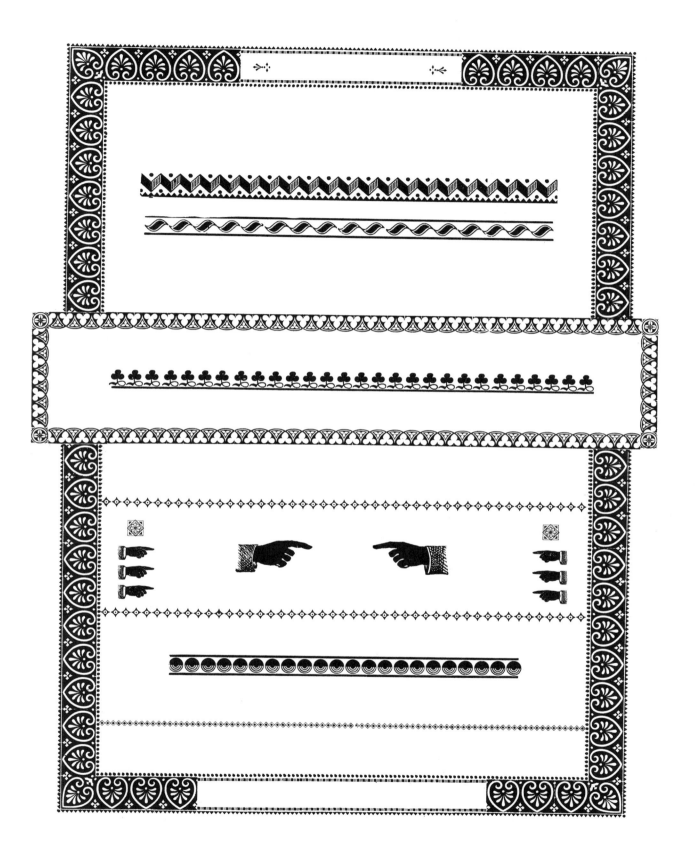

89

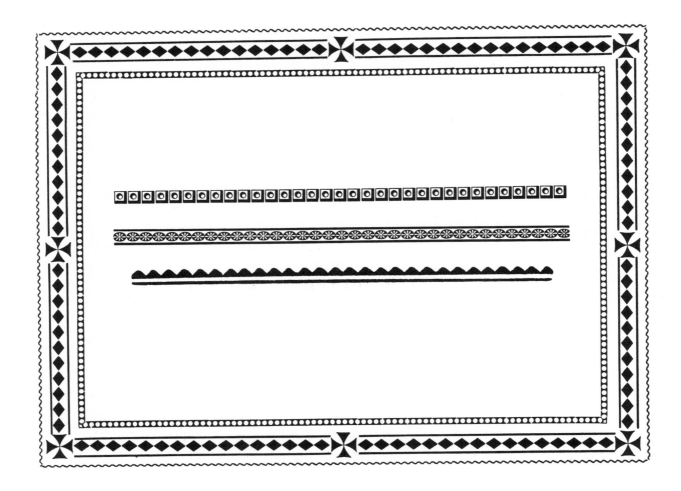

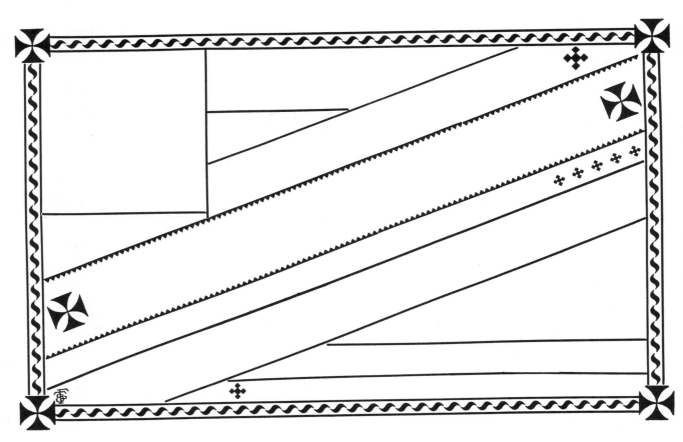

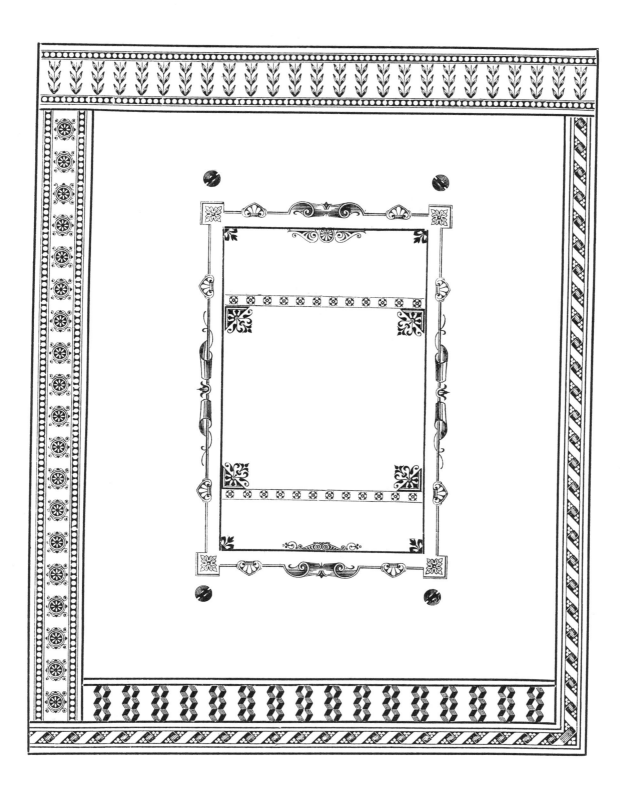

93

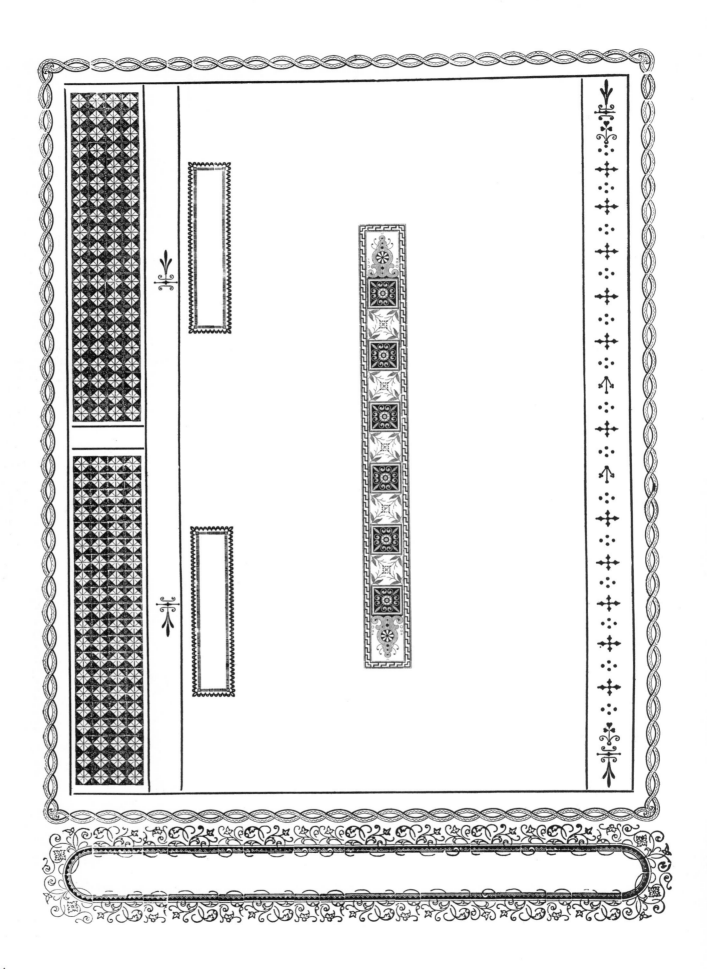

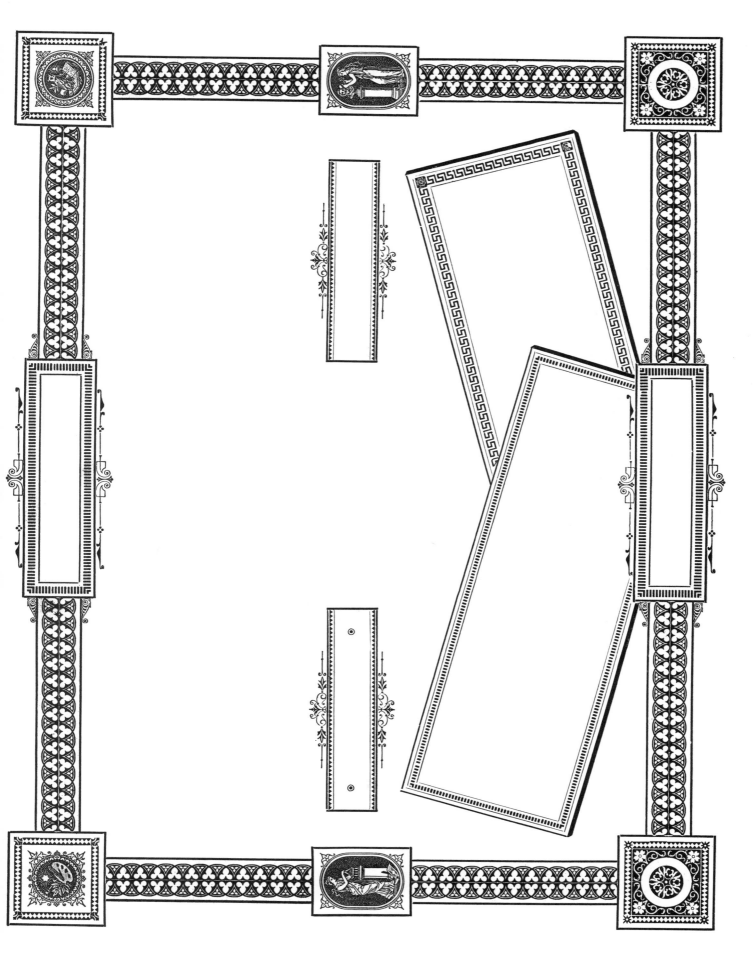

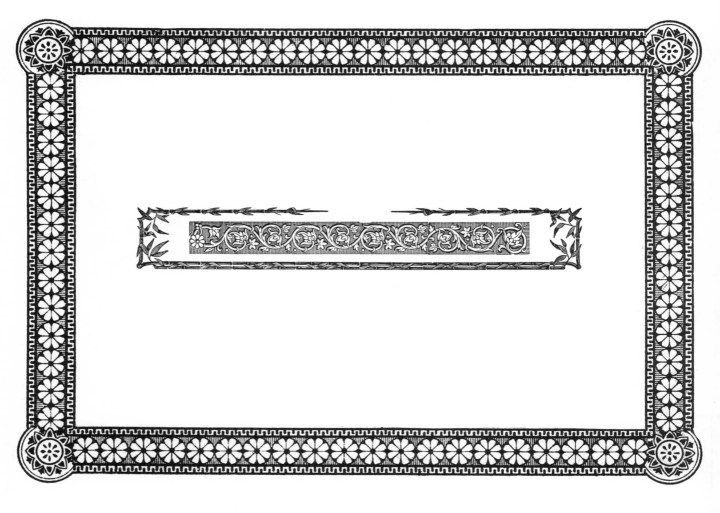

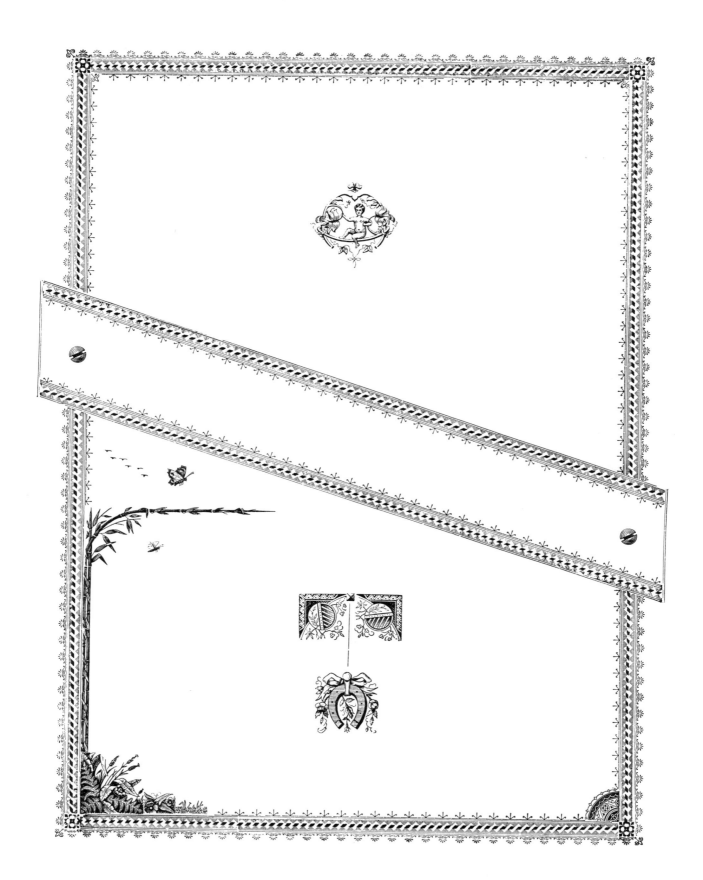

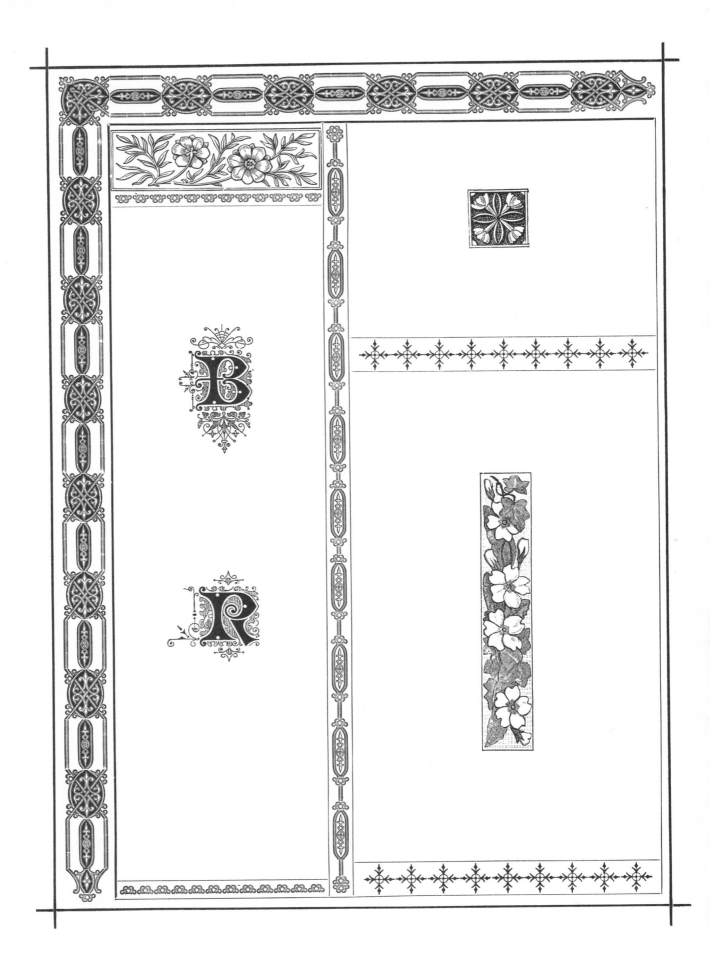

100

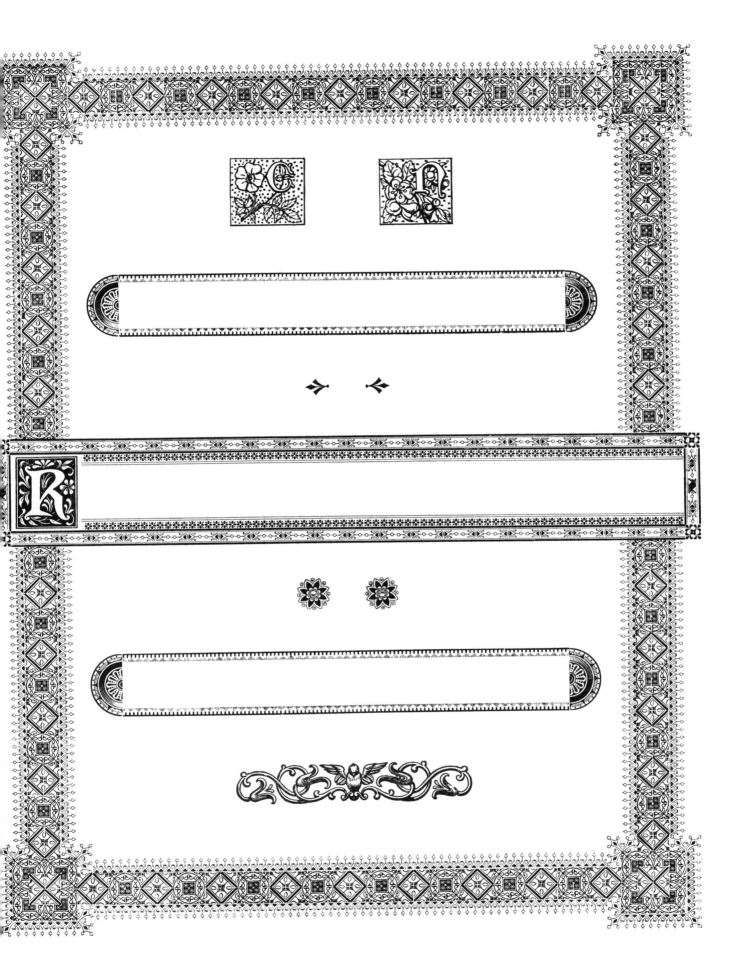

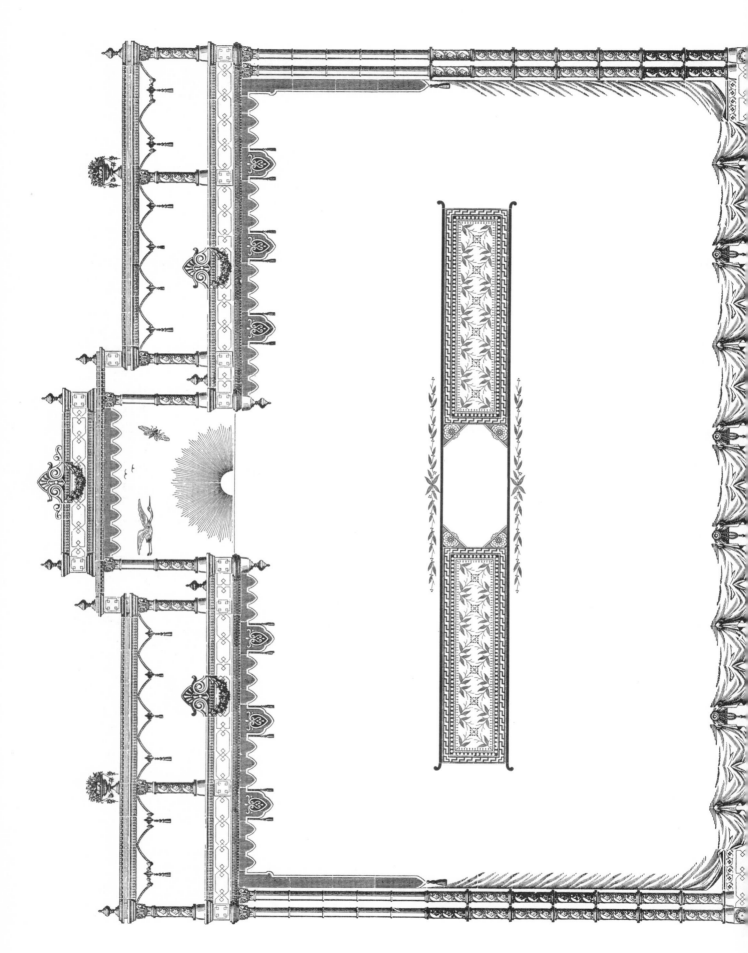

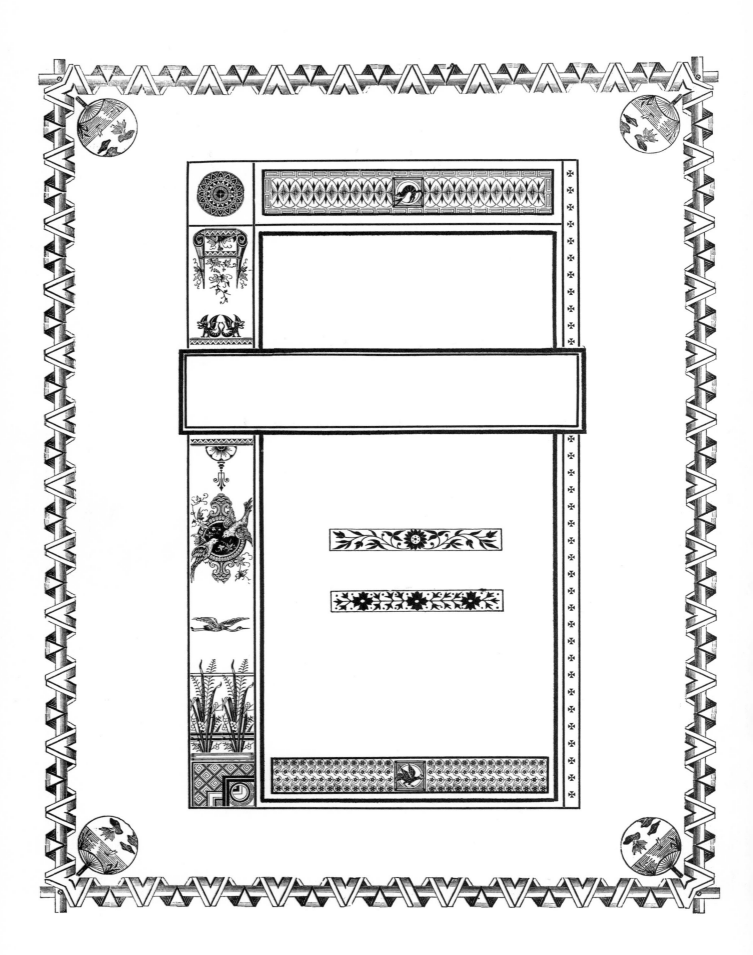

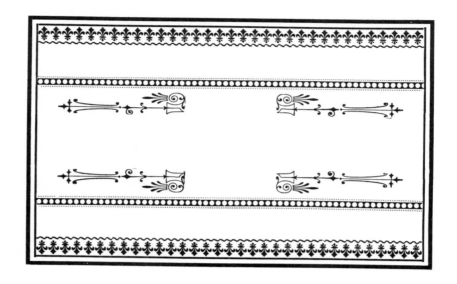

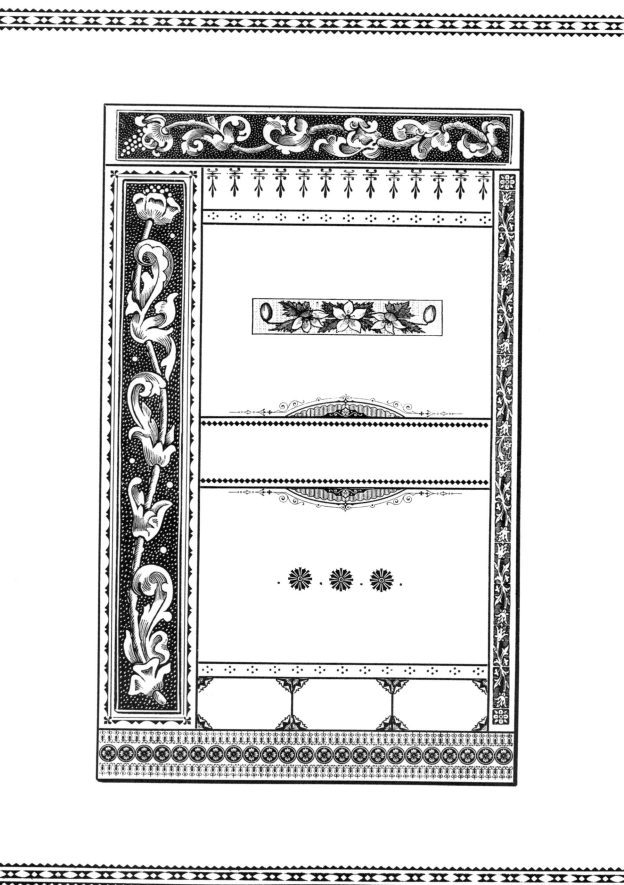

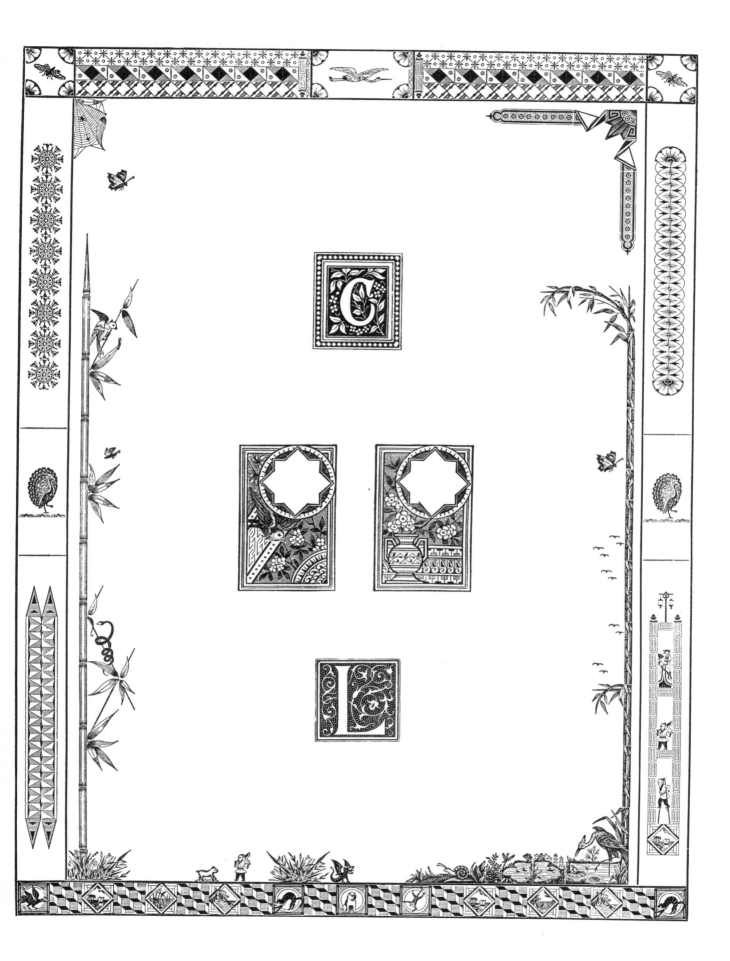

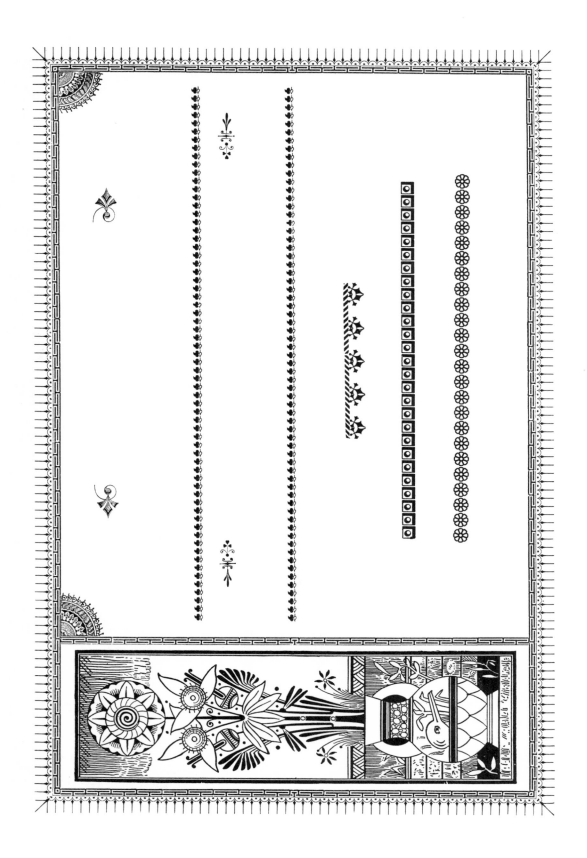

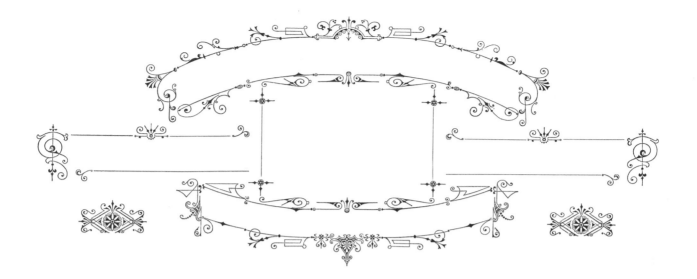

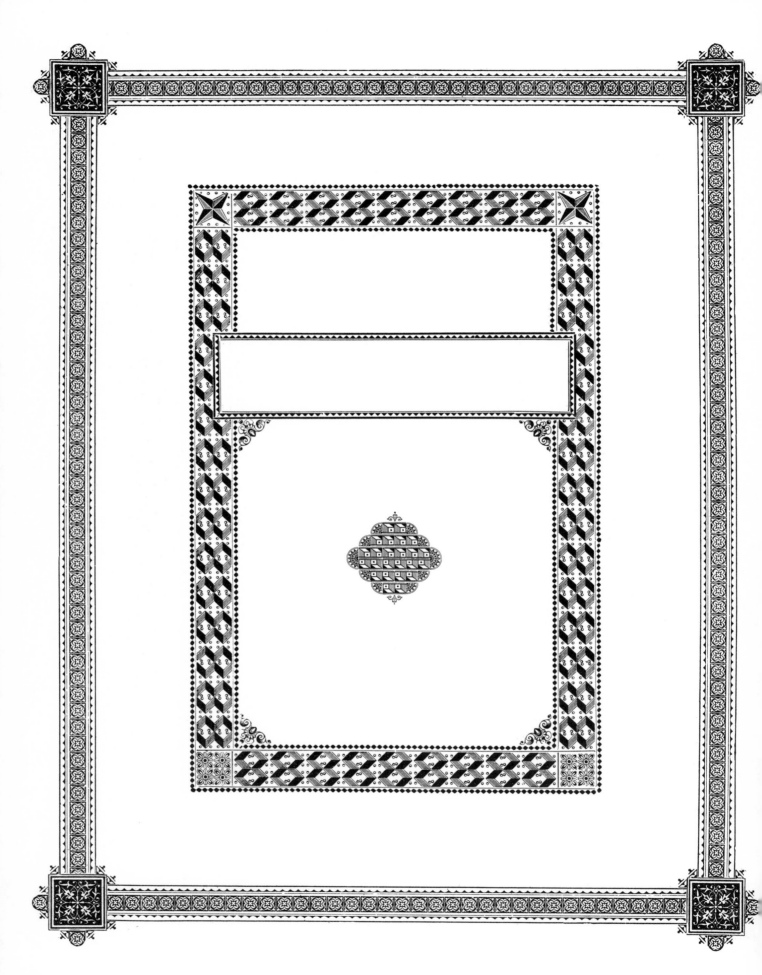

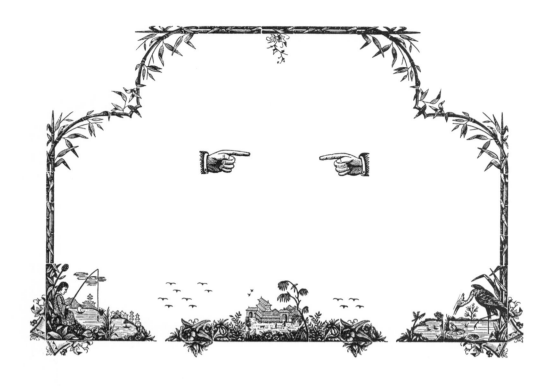

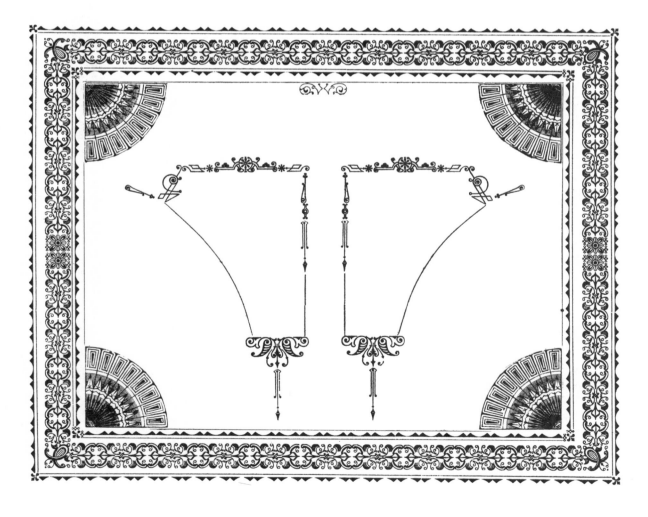

118

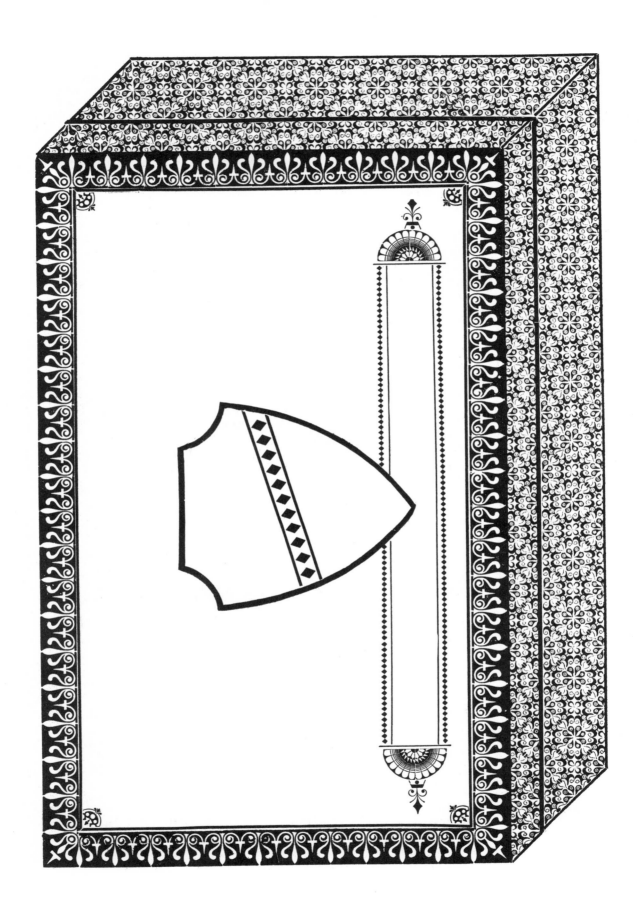